Corsica Travel Guide 2024

Discover Corsica: A Journey through Timeless Beauty, Culinary Riches, and Unforgettable Adventures – Your Essential Travel Companion for 2024

MICKEY ALLEN

Contents

1. Introduction

Welcome to Corsica: A Tapestry of Timeless Beauty and Rich Heritage

Embark on a journey to Corsica, where rugged mountains meet the azure Mediterranean, and the air is imbued with the essence of adventure. As you prepare to explore this enchanting island, let this introduction be your compass, guiding you through the tapestry of Corsican culture, history, and practicalities.

A Mosaic of Cultures and Traditions: Corsica, an island nestled between France and Italy, boasts a rich cultural heritage shaped by centuries of influences. The Corsican people, proud and resilient, have preserved their unique identity while embracing the tapestry of Mediterranean and European cultures. In the heart of Corsican culture is the emphasis on family, community, and a deep connection to the island's breathtaking landscapes.

A Glimpse into Corsican History: Corsica's history is a tale of resilience, independence, and cultural evolution. From ancient times through

Genoese and Pisan rule to French annexation, each chapter has woven a distinctive thread into the island's narrative. Ruins of ancient fortresses stand as silent witnesses to Corsica's storied past, and every cobblestone street whispers tales of the struggles and triumphs that have shaped this island into the gem it is today.

A Melting Pot of Faiths: Corsica's religious landscape is a testament to its diverse history. While the majority of Corsicans adhere to Roman Catholicism, the island also welcomes other religious expressions. The harmony of churches, chapels, and religious festivals reflects the coexistence of different faiths, creating a spiritual mosaic that adds depth to the cultural experience.

Navigating the Corsican Currency: Prepare to delve into the Corsican way of life by familiarizing yourself with the currency. The Euro is the official currency on the island, ensuring a seamless experience when indulging in the vibrant local markets, charming boutiques, and delectable eateries. So, don't forget to carry some Euros as you immerse yourself in the island's offerings.

Laws and Customs: Understanding local laws and customs is essential for a smooth and enjoyable visit. While Corsica is an integral part of France, it holds a degree of autonomy, reflected in its unique legal system. Visitors are encouraged to respect the environment, adhere to conservation guidelines, and engage with the community with an open heart. Whether navigating the charming villages or exploring the pristine nature reserves, a mindful approach to local customs ensures a harmonious connection with the island.

As you prepare to set foot on Corsican soil, envision the warmth of the sun, the fragrance of the maquis, and the echo of centuries-old stories carried by the gentle breeze. This guide is your key to unlocking the secrets of Corsica, an island where the past and present dance together, inviting you to become a part of its enchanting tale. So, pack your sense of wonder and embark on a journey through the heart of Corsica – where every cobblestone has a story to tell, and every sunset paints a new chapter in the canvas of your travel adventure.

2. Planning Your Trip

Best Time to Visit Corsica

Corsica, with its diverse landscapes and Mediterranean climate, offers a unique experience throughout the year. Choosing the right time to visit can significantly enhance your overall enjoyment of this beautiful island. Here's a guide to help you plan the perfect timing for your Corsican adventure:

1. **Summer (June to August):**

    -   *Peak Tourist Season:* The summer months attract the most visitors due to warm temperatures and long, sunny days.

    -   *Beach Bliss:* Ideal for beach lovers, with crystal-clear waters and numerous water activities.

    -   *Festivals and Events:* Many local festivals, cultural events, and outdoor concerts take place during this vibrant season.

2. **Spring (April to May) and Fall (September to October):**

- *Mild Weather:* Enjoy pleasant temperatures, making it an excellent time for outdoor activities without the summer crowds.

- *Blooming Nature:* Spring brings colorful wildflowers, while fall showcases the changing colors of the landscape.

- *Hiking Paradise:* Perfect for hiking enthusiasts as the trails are less crowded, and the weather remains comfortable.

3. **Winter (November to March):**

- *Quiet Retreat:* Corsica is less crowded during the winter months, providing a tranquil escape for those seeking solitude.

- *Snow-Capped Mountains:* Winter is the time for snow enthusiasts, with opportunities for skiing and snowboarding in the mountainous regions.

- *Festive Season:* Experience Corsican culture during the festive season with unique traditions and local celebrations.

Pro Tips:

- **Avoiding Crowds:** If you prefer a quieter experience, consider visiting in the shoulder seasons of spring or fall when the weather is still pleasant, and popular attractions are less crowded.

- **Specific Activities:** Plan your visit based on the activities you're interested in. Summer for beach lovers, spring and fall for hiking and exploring, and winter for a unique winter sports experience.

Whether you're looking for a lively summer vacation or a serene winter retreat, Corsica has something to offer year-round. Consider your preferences and the activities you'd like to engage in when deciding the best time to explore this enchanting island.

Visa Requirements and Travel Essentials

Before embarking on your journey to Corsica, it's crucial to ensure that you have all the necessary documents and travel essentials in order. Here's a comprehensive guide to help you navigate through visa requirements and essential preparations:

1. Visa Requirements:

- **EU Citizens:** If you're a citizen of a European Union (EU) member state, you can travel to Corsica without a visa. However, it's advisable to carry a valid ID card or passport for identification purposes.

- **Non-EU Citizens:** Visitors from non-EU countries may require a visa. Check with the French consulate or embassy in your home country for specific visa requirements and application procedures.

2. Passport Validity:

- Ensure that your passport is valid for at least three months beyond your intended departure date from Corsica.

3. Travel Insurance:

- It's highly recommended to have comprehensive travel insurance covering medical emergencies, trip cancellations, and lost or stolen belongings.

4. Currency and Banking:

- The official currency is the Euro (EUR). Inform your bank about your travel dates to avoid any issues with card transactions. ATMs are widely available for cash withdrawals.

5. Language:

- While French is the official language, many Corsicans speak Corsican, and English is commonly spoken in tourist areas. It's helpful to learn some basic

French phrases for smoother communication.

6. Health Precautions:

- Check if any vaccinations are required before traveling to Corsica. Carry necessary medications, and be aware of the location of medical facilities on the island.

7. Electricity:

- Corsica uses the standard European two-pin plugs, with a voltage of 230V and a frequency of 50Hz. Make sure to bring the appropriate adapter for your electronic devices.

8. Climate-Appropriate Clothing:

- Pack clothing suitable for the season of your visit. Summers can be hot, so lightweight clothing is essential, while winters may require warmer layers, especially if you plan to explore the mountainous areas.

9. Local Customs and Etiquette:

- Familiarize yourself with Corsican customs, such as greetings and dining etiquette, to show respect for the local culture.

10. Emergency Numbers and Contacts:

- Save local emergency numbers and the contact information of your country's embassy or consulate in case of any unforeseen circumstances.

By taking care of these visa requirements and travel essentials, you'll set the foundation for a smooth and enjoyable visit to Corsica. Always stay informed and prepared to make the most of your travel experience.

Transportation Options and Getting Around the Island

Corsica's diverse landscapes and charming towns are best explored with a well-thought-out transportation plan. Here's a guide to the various transportation options available, ensuring you can navigate the island with ease:

1. **Car Rental:**

   - **Recommended for Exploration:** Renting a car is arguably the best way to explore Corsica, especially if you want the freedom to discover remote areas and picturesque landscapes.

   - **Rental Agencies:** Numerous car rental agencies operate at airports and major towns. It's advisable to book in advance, especially during peak seasons.

2. **Public Transportation:**

   - **Buses:** Corsica has an extensive bus network connecting major towns and cities. While buses are a cost-effective option, they might not reach more remote areas.

- **Trains:** The train system links some key destinations, offering scenic routes through the island. Check the schedule and routes to see if it aligns with your travel plans.

3. **Taxis and Ride-Sharing:**

- **Taxis:** Taxis are available in urban areas and can be hailed or pre-booked. They are convenient for shorter distances and can also be hired for day trips.

- **Ride-Sharing Apps:** Ride-sharing services may be available in larger towns. Check local apps or international services for convenient transportation.

4. **Ferry Services:**

- **Inter-Island Travel:** Corsica is well-connected by ferry services, allowing you to explore neighboring islands like Sardinia and mainland France.

- **Car Ferries:** If you're traveling with a car, consider taking a car ferry for more flexibility in exploring the island.

5. **Domestic Flights:**

- **Limited Airports:** Corsica has a few airports, and domestic flights can be an efficient way to cover longer distances quickly.

- **Island-Hopping:** Internal flights can also facilitate island-hopping, allowing you to experience different regions.

6. **Cycling and Walking:**

- **Scenic Routes:** For the adventurous traveler, cycling and walking paths offer a unique perspective of Corsica's beauty. Explore the GR20 hiking trail or rent a bike to tour the island at your own pace.

7. **Navigating Mountainous Areas:**

- **Mountain Roads:** Corsica's interior is mountainous, and some roads can be challenging. If driving, ensure your vehicle is suitable for mountainous terrain, and plan routes accordingly.

Pro Tips:

- **Advance Planning:** Plan your transportation in advance, especially during peak seasons, to secure car rentals, ferry tickets, or accommodation near transportation hubs.

- **Explore Local Transportation:** Embrace local experiences by trying various transportation options, like the scenic train routes or island-hopping by ferry.

Understanding the diverse transportation options available will empower you to tailor your Corsican adventure according to your preferences and interests. Whether you prefer the freedom of a rental car or the charm of public transportation, Corsica has options for every type of traveler.

3. Top Attractions in Corsica

Must-Visit Landmarks and Historical Sites

Corsica, steeped in history and adorned with breathtaking landscapes, offers a plethora of landmarks and historical sites that transport visitors through time. Here are some essential stops to enrich your Corsican journey:

1. **Citadel of Calvi:**

   - **Historical Marvel:** Explore the well-preserved Citadel of Calvi, a medieval fortress perched on a rocky promontory. Enjoy panoramic views of the town and the Mediterranean Sea.

2. **Bonifacio Citadel:**

   - **Clifftop Elegance:** Visit the dramatic Bonifacio Citadel, perched on limestone cliffs overlooking the sparkling waters. The citadel is rich in history and provides stunning views of the Bonifacio Strait.

3. Ajaccio - Napoleon's Birthplace:

- **Cultural Heritage:** Immerse yourself in the history of Corsica's most famous son, Napoleon Bonaparte, by visiting his birthplace in Ajaccio. The Maison Bonaparte is a museum showcasing the Bonaparte family's life.

4. Corte - Citadel and Museum:

- **Corsican Heartland:** Discover the inland town of Corte, home to a historic citadel and the Museum of Corsica. Gain insights into the island's cultural and historical significance.

5. Filitosa Megalithic Site:

- **Prehistoric Wonders:** Explore Filitosa, an ancient megalithic site with mysterious stone statues dating back to prehistoric times. The site provides a glimpse into Corsica's early inhabitants.

6. Romanesque Churches:

- **Spiritual Heritage:** Corsica boasts several Romanesque churches, such as the Church of San Michele de Murato and the Church of San Pancraziu. Admire their architecture and artistic details.

7. **Genoese Towers:**

- **Coastal Guardians:** Throughout Corsica, you'll find Genoese towers that once served as coastal defenses. Visit the Tower of Mortella or the Tower of Parata for stunning views and historical significance.

8. **L'Île-Rousse - Place Paoli:**

- **Charming Square:** Experience the laid-back atmosphere of L'Île-Rousse and its central square, Place Paoli. The square is surrounded by colorful buildings, cafes, and a vibrant market.

9. **Sartène - The Most Corsican of Corsican Towns:**

- **Authentic Atmosphere:** Sartène is renowned as one of the most Corsican towns. Wander through its narrow streets, visit the Museum of Prehistory, and soak in the local atmosphere.

10. **Cap Corse - Sentinelle Tower:**

- **Scenic Peninsula:** Explore the rugged beauty of Cap Corse and visit the Sentinelle Tower for panoramic views of the coastline. Cap Corse is also known for its picturesque fishing villages.

Pro Tips:

- **Guided Tours:** Consider guided tours for in-depth insights into the history and significance of these landmarks.

- **Timing:** Some sites may have specific opening hours or seasonal closures, so plan your visits accordingly.

Corsica's rich history and diverse landscapes provide a captivating backdrop for exploration. These must-visit landmarks and historical sites promise an immersive journey into the island's cultural tapestry.

Natural Wonders and Scenic Spots

Corsica's natural beauty is nothing short of awe-inspiring, offering a tapestry of landscapes that range from pristine beaches to rugged mountains. Immerse yourself in the island's breathtaking natural wonders and scenic spots:

1. **Calanques de Piana:**

   - **Dramatic Rock Formations:** Witness the striking red granite cliffs and unique rock formations of Calanques de Piana. The contrast against the deep blue Mediterranean Sea creates a visual spectacle.

2. **Gulf of Porto - UNESCO World Heritage Site:**

   - **Marine Marvels:** Explore the Gulf of Porto, a UNESCO World Heritage Site known for its impressive rock formations and diverse marine life. Boat tours offer an unforgettable perspective of the rugged coastline.

3. **Valley of Restonica:**

   - **Alpine Serenity:** Hike through the stunning Valley of Restonica, surrounded by granite peaks, crystal-clear lakes, and dense pine forests. The turquoise waters of Lake Melu are a highlight of this alpine paradise.

4. **Bavella Needles:**

   - **Granite Spires:** Admire the jagged peaks of the Bavella Needles, a mountain range with towering granite spires. The Col de Bavella offers panoramic views of this remarkable natural wonder.

5. **Lavezzi Islands:**

   - **Underwater Paradise:** Embark on a boat trip to the Lavezzi Islands, a group of granite islands with pristine beaches and crystal-clear waters. Snorkeling enthusiasts will find a vibrant underwater world.

6. **Scandola Nature Reserve - UNESCO World Heritage Site:**

- **Untouched Wilderness:** Experience the untouched beauty of the Scandola Nature Reserve, a UNESCO World Heritage Site. This marine and terrestrial sanctuary is known for its rugged cliffs, diverse flora, and fauna.

7. **Capo Rosso:**

- **Sunset Spectacle:** Head to Capo Rosso for a mesmerizing sunset over the Gulf of Porto. The Genoese Tower adds a touch of history to the stunning coastal scenery.

8. **GR20 Hiking Trail:**

- **Challenging Adventure:** For avid hikers, the GR20 trail offers a challenging yet rewarding trek through Corsica's mountainous terrain. The route showcases diverse landscapes, from dense forests to high mountain passes.

9. **Aiguilles de Popolasca:**

- **Majestic Peaks:** Marvel at the Aiguilles de Popolasca, striking granite peaks that dominate the landscape. These majestic mountains are a testament to Corsica's geological wonders.

10. **Gorges de la Restonica:**

- **Rocky Ravines:** Explore the Gorges de la Restonica, a series of rocky ravines carved by the Restonica River. The hiking trails lead to hidden pools and waterfalls nestled within the rugged terrain.

Pro Tips:

- **Outdoor Activities:** Many natural wonders offer opportunities for activities like hiking, snorkeling, and boat tours, so pack accordingly.

- **Guided Tours:** Consider guided excursions to gain insights into the ecological significance and cultural stories behind these natural wonders.

Corsica's natural wonders and scenic spots beckon adventure seekers, nature enthusiasts, and those seeking moments of tranquility amidst stunning landscapes. Explore these gems to discover the island's untamed beauty.

Hidden Gems and Off-the-Beaten-Path Discoveries
Corsica's charm extends beyond its well-known landmarks, revealing hidden gems and off-the-beaten-path treasures that promise unique and intimate experiences. Venture off the tourist trail to discover these lesser-known wonders:

1. **Capo di Feno Beach:**

   - **Secluded Shoreline:** Escape the crowds and discover the secluded beauty of Capo di Feno Beach. This unspoiled stretch of coastline offers golden sands and turquoise waters, perfect for a tranquil day by the sea.

2. **Galeria:**

- **Riverside Oasis:** Explore Galeria, a charming village nestled along the Fango River. Enjoy the peaceful ambiance, picturesque landscapes, and the opportunity to embark on a boat trip up the river to discover hidden swimming spots.

3. **Cucuruzzu and Capula:**

- **Prehistoric Enclaves:** Unearth Corsica's prehistoric past at Cucuruzzu and Capula. These ancient stone structures, hidden in the Alta Rocca mountains, provide a glimpse into the island's rich archaeological heritage.

4. **Mare e Monti Trail:**

- **Scenic Hiking Trail:** Escape into nature on the Mare e Monti trail, a lesser-known hiking route that winds through remote villages, lush forests, and offers panoramic views of the Gulf of Porto.

5. **Vallée de l'Ortolo:**

- **Serene Valley:** Discover the tranquility of Vallée de l'Ortolo, a serene valley with charming villages like Olivese. Take leisurely strolls through the vineyards and olive groves, soaking in the authentic Corsican countryside.

6. **Chapelle de Notre-Dame de la Serra:**

- **Panoramic Sanctuary:** Ascend to the Chapelle de Notre-Dame de la Serra for breathtaking views over Calvi and its surroundings. This hidden chapel provides a peaceful retreat away from the bustling town below.

7. **Les Calanche Cliffs:**

- **Secluded Coastal Majesty:** Venture to the Les Calanche Cliffs, a quieter alternative to the more famous Piana Calanques. Marvel at the intricate rock formations and enjoy the solitude of this coastal gem.

8. **Tavignano Valley:**

   - **Verdant Ravines:** Explore the Tavignano Valley, known for its lush landscapes and charming hamlets. Hike along the riverbanks, discover waterfalls, and experience the untouched beauty of Corsica's interior.

9. **Église de San Michele de Murato:**

   - **Historic Church:** Visit the Église de San Michele de Murato, a hidden gem among Corsica's Romanesque churches. Admire the well-preserved architecture and immerse yourself in the quiet spirituality of this ancient site.

10. **Plage de Nonza:**

    - **Black Pebble Beach:** Uncover the unique beauty of Plage de Nonza, a black pebble beach near the village of Nonza. The contrast between the dark stones and the turquoise sea creates a mesmerizing scene.

Pro Tips:

- **Local Guidance:** Seek recommendations from locals or smaller tourism offices for lesser-known spots and experiences.

- **Off-Peak Exploration:** Visit these hidden gems during off-peak hours or seasons to enhance the sense of solitude and connection with nature.

Corsica's hidden gems and off-the-beaten-path discoveries promise an intimate and authentic experience, allowing travelers to connect with the island's lesser-explored but equally enchanting facets. Embrace the spirit of adventure and uncover these treasures for a truly unique Corsican journey.

4. Culinary Delights of Corsica

Introduction to Corsican Cuisine

Embarking on a gastronomic adventure in Corsica unveils a tapestry of flavors rooted in the island's rich cultural heritage and diverse landscapes. Corsican cuisine is a celebration of fresh, local ingredients and a harmonious blend of influences from Italy, France, and the Mediterranean. Prepare to indulge in a culinary journey that reflects the essence of this enchanting island.

1. **Corsican Charcuterie:**

   - **A Symphony of Cured Meats:** Corsican charcuterie is a carnivore's delight, featuring an array of cured meats. Lonzu, coppa, and figatellu take center stage, offering a medley of savory, smoky, and spicy notes. Enjoy these delicacies on their own or as part of a traditional charcuterie platter.

2. **Brocciu Cheese:**

   - **From Pasture to Plate:** Brocciu, a fresh cheese made from sheep or goat's milk, holds a special place in Corsican hearts and kitchens. Its versatility shines in savory dishes like the famed Corsican omelet, as well as in sweet treats like fiadone, a delightful cheesecake.

3. **Chestnut-Inspired Creations:**

   - **Nourishment from the Forests:** Corsican cuisine has a strong connection to the chestnut, prevalent in the island's groves. Taste the essence of the land in dishes like pulenda, a chestnut polenta, or castagnacciu, a chestnut cake, providing a unique culinary experience.

4. **Seafood Extravaganza:**

   - **Fresh Catch of the Day:** The island's coastal charm extends to its seafood offerings. Delight your palate with bouillabaisse, a rich fisherman's stew, or simply savor grilled fish showcasing the day's fresh catch. Coastal towns are perfect places to savor the maritime delights of Corsica.

5. **Wild Game Adventures:**

- **A Taste of the Maquis:** Corsican maquis, the fragrant scrubland, imparts its flavors to wild game dishes. Indulge in Corsican lamb, wild boar stews, and game birds seasoned with aromatic herbs like rosemary, myrtle, and thyme, creating a culinary ode to the island's untamed landscapes.

6. **Accenti Wine:**

- **Vineyards Amidst Beauty:** The vineyards of Corsica produce wines that are a testament to the island's terroir. Sip on Accenti wines, notably those from the Patrimonio and Ajaccio regions, where the grape varieties Niellucciu and

Vermentinu shine, complementing Corsican cuisine with finesse.

7. **Vegetarian Palette:**

- **Bounty of the Gardens:** Vegetarians, too, will find their haven in Corsican cuisine. Fresh, farm-to-table vegetables take center stage in dishes like aubergine tian and hearty vegetable soups, showcasing the island's commitment to sustainable, wholesome eating.

8. **Canistrelli Biscuits:**

- **Crunchy Confections:** Conclude your meals with canistrelli, traditional Corsican biscuits that come in various flavors. Almond canistrelli, in particular, offer a delightful crunch, making them a perfect accompaniment to Corsican coffee or a sweet ending to your culinary journey.

9. **Corsican Honey:**

- **Nature's Sweetness:** Corsican honey, infused with the aromatic essence of the maquis, provides a natural sweetness to various dishes. Whether drizzled over cheese or enjoyed with breakfast, it encapsulates the unique flavors of Corsica's diverse landscapes.

Pro Tips:

- **Local Markets:** Immerse yourself in the local food scene by exploring vibrant markets where you can discover fresh, seasonal produce and artisanal delights.

- **Cooking Classes:** Consider taking a cooking class to learn the art of Corsican cuisine and recreate the flavors back home.

Corsican cuisine is more than a meal; it's a sensory exploration of the island's history, geography, and cultural diversity. Allow your taste buds to dance through the unique flavors of Corsica, and let each bite tell you a story of this Mediterranean paradise.

Popular Local Dishes and Where to Try Them

As you journey through Corsica's culinary landscape, there are certain dishes that stand out as must-try delights. Venture beyond the ordinary and savor these Corsican specialties at local eateries and hidden gems across the island:

1. **Corsican Charcuterie - Lonzu, Coppa, Figatellu:**

   - **Where to Try:** Visit a local charcuterie shop or a traditional Corsican market to indulge in these cured meat wonders. In Ajaccio, try U Stazzu, a renowned charcuterie, or explore rural villages for authentic, family-run establishments.

2. **Brocciu Cheese Creations - Corsican Omelet (Frittata), Fiadone:**

   - **Where to Try:** Seek out family-run restaurants and agriturismi (farmhouses) for authentic brocciu experiences. In Corte, try Restaurant A Pasturella for their Corsican omelet, and for fiadone, La Vieille Cave in Bonifacio is a delightful choice.

3. **Chestnut-Inspired Dishes - Pulenda, Castagnacciu:**

   - **Where to Try:** Head to the mountainous villages, especially in Castagniccia, for chestnut-focused dishes. Auberge A Pignata in Evisa is known for its pulenda, while Chez Vincent in Bocognano offers a taste of Castagnacciu.

4. **Seafood Extravaganza - Bouillabaisse, Grilled Fish:**

   - **Where to Try:** Coastal towns like Ajaccio, Bastia, and Calvi boast seafood restaurants with ocean-fresh offerings. La Table du Pêcheur in Ajaccio is renowned for its bouillabaisse, while Le Pirate in Porto serves excellent grilled fish.

5. **Wild Game Delights - Corsican Lamb, Wild Boar Stew:**

- **Where to Try:** For Corsican lamb, La Ferme Auberge A Pignata in Evisa is a great choice. Inland villages like Zonza and Sartène offer restaurants such as Auberge du Prunelli, where you can relish hearty wild boar stews.

6. **Accenti Wine - Niellucciu, Vermentinu Varieties:**

- **Where to Try:** Explore Corsican vineyards and wineries in regions like Patrimonio and Ajaccio. Domaine Gentile in Patrimonio is acclaimed for its Niellucciu, while Clos Culombu offers excellent Vermentinu in Lumio.

7. **Vegetarian Options - Aubergine Tian, Vegetable Soups:**

- **Where to Try:** Vegetarian delights can be found in traditional Corsican restaurants and farm-to-table eateries.

Le Cosmo in Bonifacio is known for its aubergine tian, and Le Refuge in Corte offers wholesome vegetable soups.

8. **Canistrelli Biscuits:**

  - **Where to Try:** Purchase these crunchy delights at local markets, bakeries, or even supermarkets across Corsica. Biscuiterie d'Afa in Ajaccio and Maison Ceccaldi in Corte are renowned for their artisanal canistrelli.

9. **Corsican Honey:**

  - **Where to Try:** Purchase Corsican honey from local markets or specialized honey shops. In Bastia, Maison Mattei is a recommended spot to explore a variety of Corsican honeys.

Pro Tips:

  - **Ask Locals:** Don't hesitate to ask locals for recommendations; they often know the best-kept secrets for authentic and delicious dining experiences.

- **Explore Rural Villages:** Venture into the heart of Corsica's rural villages for an authentic taste of local cuisine, where family-run establishments showcase the true essence of Corsican gastronomy.

Embark on a culinary journey across Corsica, savoring these local dishes in their authentic settings. From mountain villages to coastal towns, the island's diverse culinary scene promises an array of flavors that will leave an indelible mark on your gastronomic adventure.

Dining Etiquette in Corsica:

1. **Greetings:**

   - **Casual Atmosphere:** Corsican dining is generally informal, and a friendly "Bonjour" (hello) is a polite way to start any interaction.

2. **Tipping:**

   - **Service Included:** Service charges are often included in the bill. However, rounding up or leaving small change is appreciated for excellent service.

3. **Reservations:**

   - **Advisable in Popular Spots:** Making reservations, especially in popular restaurants, is advisable, especially during peak tourist seasons.

4. **Dress Code:**

   - **Casual Elegance:** Corsicans appreciate a neat appearance, but the dress code is generally casual. However, in more upscale establishments, smart casual attire is suitable.

5. **Timing:**

   - **Leisurely Meals:** Corsican dining embraces a leisurely pace. Enjoy your meal, savor the flavors, and don't rush. It's a social experience.

Recommended Restaurants:

1. **Auberge Chez Vincent (Bocognano):**

- **Culinary Heritage:** Known for its chestnut-inspired dishes, this restaurant in Bocognano offers a cozy atmosphere and traditional Corsican flavors.

2. **La Table du Pêcheur (Ajaccio):**

- **Seafood Extravaganza:** Located in Ajaccio, this restaurant is celebrated for its bouillabaisse and a wide selection of fresh seafood dishes.

3. **Le Cosmo (Bonifacio):**

- **Vegetarian Delights:** Vegetarians will appreciate the offerings at Le Cosmo, where the aubergine tian is a standout dish. The restaurant boasts a terrace with stunning views.

4. **La Ferme Auberge A Pignata (Evisa):**

   - **Corsican Lamb:** Situated in Evisa, this farm-to-table establishment is renowned for its Corsican lamb dishes, offering an authentic mountain dining experience.

5. **Domaine Gentile (Patrimonio):**

   - **Wine Tasting Extravaganza:** For a wine-centric experience, visit Domaine Gentile in Patrimonio. Sample their Niellucciu wines amidst picturesque vineyards.

6. **Le Pirate (Porto):**

   - **Coastal Charm:** Located in Porto, Le Pirate is a seafood haven with a terrace overlooking the sea. Enjoy grilled fish and other maritime delights.

7. **Le Refuge (Corte):**

   - **Hearty Wild Boar Stews:** Nestled in Corte, Le Refuge is known for its authentic Corsican cuisine, including hearty wild boar stews and other mountain-inspired dishes.

8. **Maison Ceccaldi (Corte):**

   - **Artisanal Canistrelli:** Indulge your sweet tooth at Maison Ceccaldi in Corte, a renowned spot for artisanal canistrelli biscuits in various flavors.

9. **Biscuiterie d'Afa (Ajaccio):**

   - **Crunchy Delights:** For a delightful selection of canistrelli, visit Biscuiterie d'Afa in Ajaccio. Choose from a range of flavors to suit your preference.

10. **Maison Mattei (Bastia):**

   - **Corsican Honey Haven:** Located in Bastia, Maison Mattei is a recommended spot for exploring a variety of Corsican honeys.

Pro Tips:

- **Local Recommendations:** Ask locals or your hosts for restaurant suggestions, as they often have insights into hidden gems.

- **Regional Specialties:** Opt for restaurants that highlight regional specialties for an authentic taste of Corsican cuisine.

Corsican dining is not just about the food; it's an immersion into the island's culture and traditions. Explore these recommended restaurants to savor the diverse flavors of Corsica, and remember to embrace the unhurried, convivial atmosphere that defines the island's dining experience.

5. Outdoor Adventures in Corsica

Hiking Trails and Trekking Routes

Corsica's rugged landscapes and diverse terrain make it a paradise for outdoor enthusiasts, especially those drawn to hiking and trekking. Whether you're a seasoned hiker or a casual nature lover, the island offers a plethora of trails that lead you through majestic mountains, dense forests, and along pristine coastlines. Lace up your hiking boots and explore the beauty of Corsica on these remarkable trails:

1. **GR20:**

   - **The Legendary Trek:** The GR20 is one of Europe's most renowned long-distance hiking trails, traversing Corsica diagonally from north to south. Expect challenging terrain, stunning mountain views, and an immersive journey through the heart of the island.

2. **Mare e Monti:**

- **Coast to Mountains:** Mare e Monti, meaning "Sea and Mountains," offers a diverse trek from the Gulf of Porto to Corte. This trail combines coastal panoramas with mountainous landscapes, providing a varied and rewarding experience.

3. **Sentier de la Transhumance:**

- **Cultural and Scenic Route:** This trail follows the ancient transhumance paths, showcasing Corsica's pastoral heritage. Wander through charming villages, lush meadows, and enjoy breathtaking views of the mountains.

4. **Calanche de Piana to Girolata:**

- **Coastal Marvels:** Embark on a coastal hike from the Calanche de Piana, known for its striking red rock formations, to the secluded village of Girolata. The trail offers stunning views of the Gulf of Girolata and the Mediterranean Sea.

5. **Capu di a Veta Loop:**

- **Mountain Bliss:** For a day hike with incredible mountain scenery, explore the Capu di a Veta Loop near Vizzavona. This trail takes you through pine forests and offers panoramic views of the surrounding peaks.

6. **Cascades des Anglais:**

- **Waterfall Wonderland:** Discover the Cascades des Anglais trail near Sartène, leading to a series of picturesque waterfalls. The hike winds through lush vegetation and provides refreshing stops at natural pools.

7. **Monte Cinto:**

- **Corsica's Highest Peak:** Conquer the highest peak in Corsica, Monte Cinto. This challenging ascent rewards hikers with breathtaking views of the island's mountainous interior and distant coastlines.

8. **Valley of Restonica:**

- **Alpine Oasis:** The Valley of Restonica, near Corte, is a haven for hikers. Choose from various trails that lead to crystal-clear lakes, glacial valleys, and stunning mountain landscapes.

9. **Aiguilles de Bavella:**

- **Granite Spires:** Explore the Aiguilles de Bavella, a mountain range with towering granite spires. Hike to iconic viewpoints like the Trou de la Bombe for panoramic vistas of the Bavella Needles.

10. **Cap Corse Coastal Trail:**

- **Seaside Exploration:** Circumnavigate the northern tip of Corsica on the Cap Corse Coastal Trail. This trail combines coastal paths with charming villages, lighthouses, and captivating seascapes.

Pro Tips:

- **Trail Difficulty:** Be aware of the difficulty levels of the trails and choose routes that align with your fitness and hiking experience.

- **Seasonal Considerations:** Some trails may be impassable or challenging during certain seasons, so check the local conditions and plan accordingly.

Corsica's hiking trails cater to all levels of adventurers, offering a chance to connect with nature and experience the island's diverse landscapes. Whether you're seeking a challenging multi-day trek or a leisurely day hike, Corsica has a trail to suit your preferences and reward you with unforgettable views and experiences.

Water Activities: Beaches, Snorkeling, and Diving

With its pristine coastline and crystalline waters, Corsica beckons water enthusiasts to explore its diverse marine landscapes. From sun-drenched beaches to vibrant underwater ecosystems, the island offers an array of water activities for every taste. Dive into the refreshing waters of Corsica and discover the aquatic wonders that await:

1. Beach Bliss:

Corsica boasts an abundance of stunning beaches, each with its own unique charm. Whether you seek tranquility or lively seaside vibes, the island has a beach to suit your preferences:

- **Palombaggia Beach:**

  - **Golden Sands and Turquoise Waters:** Located near Porto-Vecchio, Palombaggia is renowned for its powdery white sands and clear turquoise waters. Relax under the Mediterranean sun or explore the nearby rocky coves.

- **Rondinara Beach:**

  - **Picture-Perfect Bay:** Rondinara, often described as one of Corsica's most beautiful beaches, features a crescent-shaped bay with fine sand and shallow, inviting waters. Ideal for families and snorkelers.

- **Santa Giulia Beach:**

    - **Shallow Lagoon:** Santa Giulia's shallow, crystal-clear lagoon makes it perfect for swimming and water sports. Paddle in the gentle waters or enjoy beachside activities against a backdrop of scenic hills.

- **Saleccia Beach:**

    - **Untouched Beauty:** Accessible by boat or a challenging hike, Saleccia is an unspoiled gem with pristine white sand and transparent waters. Experience a sense of seclusion amidst the island's natural beauty.

2. Snorkeling Paradises:

Corsica's coastal waters are a haven for snorkelers, revealing vibrant marine life and underwater landscapes:

- **Lavezzi Islands:**

  - **Underwater Wonderland:** Take a boat trip to the Lavezzi Islands, a granite archipelago, for exceptional snorkeling. Crystal-clear waters reveal a thriving underwater world with colorful fish and intricate coral formations.

- **Réserve Naturelle de Scandola:**

  - **Marine Sanctuary:** Snorkel in the UNESCO-listed Scandola Nature Reserve, where the underwater terrain is as captivating as the rugged coastline. Encounter diverse marine species in this protected marine sanctuary.

- **Girolata Bay:**

  - **Hidden Coves:** Explore the clear waters around Girolata Bay, discovering hidden coves and underwater rock formations. Snorkelers are rewarded with glimpses of marine life thriving in the pristine environment.

3. Diving Adventures:

For those seeking deeper underwater explorations, Corsica offers exceptional diving opportunities with its diverse dive sites:

- **Réserve Naturelle de Scandola:**

  - **Dramatic Underwater Scenery:** Dive into the Scandola Nature Reserve to witness the continuation of the stunning landscapes beneath the surface. Encounters with groupers, moray eels, and colorful sea fans await.

- **Les Calanche Cliffs:**

  - **Submarine Canyons:** Dive along the Les Calanche Cliffs, where underwater canyons and caves create a dramatic landscape. Keep an eye out for marine life attracted to the nutrient-rich waters.

- **La Revellata:**

  - **Wrecks and Reefs:** Explore the dive sites around La Revellata near Calvi, known for its diverse marine ecosystems, underwater caves, and the possibility of encountering shipwrecks.

Pro Tips:

- **Equipment Rental:** If you don't have your own gear, various coastal towns and diving centers offer equipment rental for snorkeling and diving.

- **Guided Tours:** Consider joining guided snorkeling or diving tours for insights into the best spots and safety precautions.

Whether you're basking in the sun on Corsica's beautiful beaches, snorkeling in clear lagoons, or delving into the island's underwater realms through diving adventures, the water activities here promise an immersive and unforgettable experience. Dive into Corsica's aquatic wonders and let the Mediterranean sea cast its spell on you.

Adventure Sports and Outdoor Excursions

Corsica, with its diverse landscapes, invites thrill-seekers to explore the island through a variety of adventure sports and outdoor excursions. Whether you're drawn to the heights of mountain peaks or the rush of rivers, Corsica offers a playground for adrenaline enthusiasts. Embark on these heart-pounding activities to elevate your outdoor adventure in Corsica:

1. Canyoning:

- **Navigate Dramatic Gorges:** Delve into Corsica's rugged interior by trying canyoning, a thrilling activity that involves descending through narrow gorges, rappelling down waterfalls, and swimming through natural pools. The island's canyons, such as Richiusa Canyon near Corte, provide an exhilarating experience surrounded by stunning landscapes.

2. Rock Climbing:

- **Scale Granite Walls:** Corsica's granite peaks provide an excellent playground for rock climbing enthusiasts. The Bavella Massif is a renowned destination for climbing, offering routes for various skill levels. The challenging ascents reward climbers with panoramic views of the Corsican mountains.

3. Via Ferrata:

- **Cliffside Adventure:** Experience the thrill of climbing along Corsica's cliffside routes with via ferrata excursions. The Via Ferrata di L'Arche de Corte offers a unique perspective of the Restonica Valley as you traverse iron ladders and bridges anchored to the rock.

4. Paragliding:

- **Soar Above Corsica's Beauty:** Take to the skies with paragliding adventures, offering breathtaking views of Corsica's coastline and mountains. Launch from sites like Col de Bavella or Calvi and experience the island's landscapes from a perspective reserved for the brave.

5. Horseback Riding:

- **Explore Corsica on Horseback:** Discover Corsica's beauty at a leisurely pace by exploring its trails on horseback. Riding excursions allow you to connect with nature, traverse diverse landscapes, and experience the island's rural charm. Equestrian centers near Calvi and Porto-Vecchio offer guided horseback rides.

6. Mountain Biking:

- **Trail Adventures:** Corsica's varied terrain is a mountain biker's dream. Traverse forested trails, mountain paths, and coastal routes for an adrenaline-pumping ride. The GR20, though famous for hiking, also offers challenging sections for mountain biking enthusiasts.

7. Kayaking and Rafting:

- **Conquer Corsica's Rivers:** Navigate Corsica's rivers for a wet and wild adventure. Try kayaking or rafting on rivers like the Golo and Tavignano. These excursions offer a mix of adrenaline and scenic beauty as you paddle through Corsica's lush landscapes.

8. Ziplining:

- **Fly Over Canyons:** Experience the thrill of ziplining across Corsica's canyons and valleys. The Zipline de la Spelunca near Porto allows you to soar above the spectacular Spelunca Gorge, providing a unique and exhilarating perspective of the landscape.

9. Quad Biking:

- **Off-Road Exploration:** Embark on an off-road adventure with quad biking excursions. Navigate through Corsica's diverse terrain, from dense forests to open plains, for an adrenaline-fueled exploration of the island's natural beauty.

10. Sailing and Windsurfing: - **Seafaring Adventures:** Take advantage of Corsica's coastal beauty by engaging in water sports such as sailing and windsurfing. The Gulf of Porto and the Bay of Calvi are popular spots for sailing enthusiasts, while the island's varied wind conditions make it ideal for windsurfing.

Pro Tips:

- **Professional Guides:** For activities like canyoning, rock climbing, and via ferrata, consider hiring professional guides to ensure safety and enhance your experience.

- **Seasonal Considerations:** Check the best seasons for specific adventure sports, as conditions may vary throughout the year.

Corsica's rugged terrain and diverse environments set the stage for a thrilling array of adventure sports and outdoor excursions. Whether you prefer the heights of the mountains, the rush of the rivers, or the beauty of the coastline, Corsica promises an adventure-filled escape for those seeking an adrenaline boost in the great outdoors.

6. Cultural Celebrations in Corsica

Local Festivals and Events

Corsica's vibrant cultural scene comes alive with an array of festivals and events that showcase the island's rich heritage, music, dance, and traditions. Immerse yourself in the lively atmosphere of these celebrations, where locals and visitors come together to revel in the unique spirit of Corsica:

1. Festival de Calvi:

- **Musical Extravaganza:** Held in the picturesque town of Calvi, this music festival transforms the streets and squares into stages for a diverse range of performances. From classical music to contemporary sounds, Festival de Calvi attracts both local and international artists, creating a magical ambiance against the backdrop of the Calvi Citadel.

2. Les Rencontres de Calenzana:

- **Cultural Encounters:** This cultural festival in Calenzana is a celebration of Corsican arts and traditions. Visitors can enjoy traditional music, dance, and exhibitions that highlight the island's cultural richness. The festival provides a platform for local artists to showcase their talents.

3. Polyphonies de Calvi:

- **Choral Harmony:** Experience the hauntingly beautiful polyphonic singing traditions of Corsica at the Polyphonies de Calvi. Renowned choirs and vocal groups gather to perform traditional Corsican polyphony, creating an immersive experience for music enthusiasts.

4. Fiera di u Vinu:

- **Wine Celebration:** Wine lovers shouldn't miss the Fiera di u Vinu, an annual wine fair held in Luri. Celebrating Corsican viticulture, this event offers the opportunity to taste a wide array of local wines, including the island's distinct grape varieties.

5. Festimaiu:

- **May Festival:** Festimaiu is a May festival celebrated across Corsica, marking the arrival of spring. Expect lively processions, traditional music, and colorful festivities as communities come together to welcome the warmer season.

6. A Filetta Festival:

- **Vocal Harmony:** A Filetta, one of Corsica's most renowned polyphonic vocal groups, hosts an annual festival dedicated to celebrating Corsican polyphony. The event attracts polyphonic choirs from around the world, creating a harmonious celebration of this unique musical heritage.

7. Festival du Film:

- **Cinematic Showcase:** The Festival du Film in Porto-Vecchio showcases the best of Corsican and international cinema. Film enthusiasts can enjoy screenings, discussions, and the chance to explore the world of cinema against the stunning backdrop of Porto-Vecchio.

8. Sant'Andria in Ajaccio:

- **Patron Saint Celebration:** Sant'Andria, the patron saint of Ajaccio, is honored with a vibrant celebration in late November. The festivities include processions, religious ceremonies, and traditional Corsican music, offering a glimpse into the island's religious and cultural heritage.

9. Cargèse Music Festival:

- **Classical Notes by the Sea:** This classical music festival in the coastal village of Cargèse brings together talented musicians for a series of concerts. Enjoy performances in unique venues, including churches and open-air spaces, against the backdrop of the Mediterranean Sea.

10. Porto Latino Festival: - Eclectic Music Vibes: Held in Saint-Florent, the Porto Latino Festival is a music extravaganza featuring a diverse lineup of

artists. From Latin beats to international sounds, the festival attracts music enthusiasts seeking a lively atmosphere and beachside performances.

Pro Tips:

- **Check Event Dates:** Verify the dates of festivals and events, as they may vary from year to year.

- **Local Participation:** Engage with locals to learn more about smaller, community-based celebrations and events happening during your visit.

Corsica's festivals and events offer a glimpse into the island's soul, where traditions, music, and cultural heritage converge. Whether you're drawn to the melodic tunes of Corsican polyphony, the cinematic allure of film festivals, or the lively atmosphere of wine fairs, attending these celebrations adds a colorful dimension to your Corsican experience.

Traditional Music, Dance, and Art

Corsica's cultural tapestry is woven with the threads of traditional music, dance, and art, reflecting the island's unique history and diverse influences. Dive into the captivating world of Corsican culture, where ancient melodies, intricate dances, and local artistry come together to narrate the story of this Mediterranean gem:

1. Corsican Polyphony:

- **Harmony of Voices:** Corsican polyphony stands as one of the island's most iconic musical traditions. Characterized by multipart singing without instrumental accompaniment, the harmonies evoke the rugged landscapes and deep emotions of Corsica. Attend live performances or explore local gatherings to experience the enchanting power of polyphonic voices.

2. Cetera and Paghjella:

- **Ancient Melodies:** Cetera, a traditional Corsican guitar, accompanies the Paghjella, a distinctive form of polyphonic singing. The Paghjella's mournful tunes often depict tales of love, nature, and Corsican history. Delve into the soulful melodies of these ancient musical expressions during local performances or cultural events.

3. Saltarello Dance:

- **Rhythmic Revelry:** The Saltarello, a lively folk dance, captures the joyful spirit of Corsican celebrations. Dancers, clad in traditional attire, move to the energetic beats of local instruments like the diatonic accordion. Participate in local festivities or seek out performances to witness the rhythmic revelry of the Saltarello.

4. Corsican Instrumental Music:

- **Sounds of the Island:** Beyond vocal harmonies, Corsican music features traditional instruments like the Pifana (shawm) and Caramusa (bagpipes). These instruments add a distinct flavor to the island's musical heritage. Attend concerts or explore local music festivals to appreciate the diverse sounds of Corsican instrumental music.

5. Corsican Visual Arts:

- **Inspired Creations:** Corsican visual arts draw inspiration from the island's landscapes and cultural heritage. Local artists often create pieces that reflect the rugged beauty of Corsica, incorporating elements like maquis, mountains, and coastal scenes. Visit galleries and artisan markets to discover paintings, sculptures, and crafts that capture the essence of the island.

6. Traditional Crafts:

- **Artisanal Excellence:** Corsica takes pride in its traditional crafts, with artisans skillfully producing items like knives, pottery, and textiles. Explore markets in towns like Corte and Bonifacio to find handcrafted treasures that showcase the island's artistic craftsmanship.

7. Corsican Language and Literature:

- **Verbal Heritage:** The Corsican language, a Romance language with Italian and French influences, is an integral part of the island's cultural identity. Corsican literature, both oral and written, tells tales of the island's history and traditions. Engage with locals to discover the beauty of the Corsican language and explore literature that reflects the island's narratives.

8. Festive Processions:

- **Living Art:** Traditional festivals and religious processions often feature locals adorned in traditional costumes, showcasing the artistry of Corsican attire. Intricately embroidered vests, headdresses, and accessories contribute to the visual richness of these festive events.

9. Corsican Cuisine as Art:

- **Culinary Creations:** Corsican cuisine, with its emphasis on local, fresh ingredients, is a form of artistic expression. From beautifully presented dishes to the craft of charcuterie and cheese making, Corsican culinary traditions showcase the island's commitment to gastronomic artistry.

10. Museums and Cultural Centers: - Exploring Heritage:

Visit museums and cultural centers across Corsica, such as the Museu di a Corsica in Corte, to delve deeper into the island's cultural heritage. These institutions often feature exhibitions on traditional music, dance, art, and the historical development of Corsican identity.

Pro Tips:

- **Participate in Workshops:** Some cultural centers and local artisans offer workshops where visitors can engage in traditional craft activities or learn the art of Corsican polyphony.

- **Attend Local Festivals:** Many traditional music and dance performances take place during local festivals and celebrations. Check the event calendar to align your visit with these cultural showcases.

Embark on a cultural journey through Corsica, where traditional music, dance, and art weave a narrative that spans generations. Immerse yourself in the rhythms, melodies, and visual expressions that form the heartbeat of Corsican identity, and witness the island's living artistry unfold before your eyes.

Interaction with Locals and Cultural Etiquette
Corsica's warmth extends beyond its Mediterranean climate to the hospitality of its people. Engaging with locals provides a deeper understanding of the island's rich culture and traditions. To make the most of your interactions and to respect Corsican customs, consider the following cultural etiquette tips:

1. Greetings:

- **Politeness Matters:** Begin conversations with a warm "Bonjour" (good morning) or "Bonsoir" (good evening), depending on the time of day. Politeness is highly valued in Corsican culture, so adding a simple greeting goes a long way.

2. Personal Space:

- **Respectful Distances:** Corsicans appreciate a comfortable personal space. While conversations are animated and friendly, be mindful of physical proximity, especially with new acquaintances.

3. Language:

- **Learn Basic Phrases:** While many Corsicans speak French, the Corsican language (Corsu) holds cultural significance. Learning a few basic phrases in Corsican, such as "Bonghjornu" for good morning, is a gesture that locals often appreciate.

4. Respect for Traditions:

- **Observe Cultural Customs:** Corsicans take pride in their traditions. If you encounter local events, processions, or ceremonies, observe quietly and respectfully. Seek permission before taking photographs during religious or private events.

5. Dining Etiquette:

- **Leisurely Dining:** Meals in Corsica are more than sustenance; they are social events. Embrace the unhurried pace of dining, savoring each course and engaging in conversation. It's common to linger over a meal, so relax and enjoy the experience.

6. Buying Local:

- **Supporting Artisans:** When purchasing souvenirs or goods, consider buying directly from local artisans and markets. This not only ensures authenticity but also supports the island's traditional crafts and businesses.

7. Attire:

- **Casual Elegance:** Corsican attire is generally casual, but cleanliness and neatness are valued. In more formal settings or religious places, consider dressing slightly more formally, especially if attending events like festivals or processions.

8. Offer a Friendly "Salute":

- **Raise Your Glass:** Sharing a drink is a significant part of Corsican socializing. When offered a drink, it's customary to reciprocate with a friendly "Salute" (Cheers!) and make eye contact during the toast.

9. Asking for Directions:

- **Polite Inquiry:** If you need directions or assistance, approach locals with a polite "Scusatemi" (Excuse me) before asking for help. Corsicans are generally friendly and willing to offer guidance.

10. Respect Nature: - Preserve the Environment:
Corsicans have a deep connection to their natural surroundings. Whether exploring trails, beaches, or villages, practice responsible tourism by respecting the environment, disposing of waste properly, and treading lightly.

Pro Tips:

- **Engage in Conversations:** Corsicans are known for their friendliness. Strike up conversations with locals, whether at a café, market, or during cultural events. Sharing experiences and asking for recommendations can lead to memorable encounters.

- **Adapt to Local Rhythms:** Corsica operates on its own time, especially in smaller towns and villages. Embrace the relaxed pace, and don't be surprised if things move a bit slower than in more bustling destinations.

By embracing Corsican customs and demonstrating respect for local traditions, you'll find that the island's residents are welcoming and eager to share their culture with visitors. Approach interactions with an open heart, and you'll likely forge connections that enhance your Corsican experience.

7. Practical Tips for a Smooth Stay in Corsica

Currency, Banking, and Communication

Navigating the practical aspects of your stay in Corsica, including currency matters, banking services, and communication, is crucial for a seamless travel experience. Here's a guide to help you manage these essential aspects during your visit:

1. Currency:

- **Euro (EUR):** The official currency of Corsica is the Euro. Ensure you have sufficient cash for small purchases and transactions, especially in rural areas and local markets where card payments may not be as prevalent.

2. Banking Services:

- **ATMs and Banks:** Corsica is equipped with ATMs (Automated Teller Machines) in major towns and cities, providing convenient access to cash. Banking hours typically run from Monday to Friday, and some banks may close for a few hours during lunchtime.

- **Credit and Debit Cards:** Major credit and debit cards (Visa, MasterCard, etc.) are widely accepted in larger establishments such as hotels, restaurants, and shops. However, it's advisable to carry some cash, particularly in smaller villages and for services like taxis.

- **Currency Exchange:** While larger towns may have currency exchange services, it's recommended to exchange currency at banks or withdraw cash from ATMs for better rates.

3. Communication:

- **Languages Spoken:** French is the official language, and it's widely spoken across the island. Corsican (Corsu), an Italian-influenced Romance language, is also spoken by locals. In tourist areas, you'll find that many people speak English, especially in hospitality and service industries.

- **Local Phrases:** Learning a few basic French or Corsican phrases can enhance your interactions with locals and demonstrate cultural respect. Phrases like "Bonjour" (hello), "Merci" (thank you), and "S'il vous plaît" (please) are useful.

- **Emergency Numbers:** The emergency number for police, medical, or fire assistance in Corsica is 112. Keep this number handy for any unforeseen situations.

- **Mobile Network Coverage:** Corsica has reliable mobile network coverage, especially in urban areas. Check with your mobile provider about international roaming plans or consider purchasing a local SIM card for your stay.

- **Internet Access:** Wi-Fi is available in most hotels, cafes, and public spaces in urban areas. However, in more remote locations, the availability of Wi-Fi may be limited. It's advisable to check with your accommodation for details on internet access.

4. Time Zone:

- **Central European Time (CET):** Corsica operates on Central European Time, which is UTC+1. The island observes Daylight Saving Time, shifting to Central European Summer Time (CEST) in the summer months (UTC+2).

5. Electrical Outlets:

- **European Standard:** The standard voltage in Corsica is 230V, and the frequency is 50Hz. The electrical outlets are of Type C and Type E, which are the standard European plug types. If your devices use a different plug, consider bringing a travel adapter.

6. Postal Services:

- **Post Offices:** Corsica has post offices in major towns, offering postal and shipping services. Check post office hours, as they may vary depending on the location.

7. Transportation Information:

- **Public Transportation:** Corsica has a network of buses and trains connecting major towns and cities. Car rentals are also popular for exploring the island's diverse landscapes. Consider renting a vehicle to access remote areas and picturesque viewpoints.

Pro Tips:

- **Cash Reserves:** While cards are widely accepted, having some cash on hand is advisable for transactions in smaller establishments or markets.

- **Check with Your Bank:** Before traveling, inform your bank about your trip to avoid any potential issues with card transactions abroad.

- **Local SIM Card:** If you rely on mobile data, consider purchasing a local SIM card for better connectivity, especially in more rural areas.

Navigating the practical aspects of your stay in Corsica ensures a smooth and enjoyable travel experience.

From managing currency to staying connected, these practical tips will help you make the most of your time on this enchanting Mediterranean island.

Health and Safety Precautions

Ensuring your well-being during your visit to Corsica is paramount. Familiarizing yourself with health and safety precautions will contribute to a secure and enjoyable travel experience on this picturesque island. Here are guidelines to prioritize your health and safety:

1. Travel Insurance:

- **Comprehensive Coverage:** Before embarking on your journey, obtain comprehensive travel insurance that covers medical emergencies, trip cancellations, and potential evacuation needs. Confirm that the policy includes coverage for outdoor activities and adventure sports if you plan to engage in such activities.

2. Emergency Services:

- **Medical Assistance:** Corsica has a well-equipped healthcare system with hospitals and medical facilities in major towns. The emergency number for medical assistance is 15. Ensure you have the contact information for local medical services, and don't hesitate to seek help if needed.

- **Pharmacies:** Pharmacies (pharmacies or "pharmacie" in French) are available in towns and cities. Keep a list of any essential medications you may need and their generic names. Pharmacies can provide over-the-counter remedies for common ailments.

- **Police and Emergency Services:** The emergency number for police, medical, or fire assistance is 112. This centralized number is applicable throughout the European Union.

3. Personal Safety:

- **Vigilance in Public Spaces:** Corsica is generally safe, but it's essential to remain vigilant, especially in crowded areas or tourist spots, to avoid pickpocketing or petty theft.

- **Weather Precautions:** Be aware of Corsica's diverse landscapes, and take necessary precautions when engaging in outdoor activities. Stay informed about weather conditions, particularly if you plan to explore mountainous or coastal areas.

4. COVID-19 Considerations:

- **Check Travel Restrictions:** Stay informed about travel restrictions and entry requirements related to COVID-19. Regulations may change, so regularly check official sources for updates.

- **Follow Health Guidelines:** Adhere to health guidelines issued by local authorities and establishments. This may include mask-wearing, social distancing, and hygiene practices.

- **Vaccinations:** Ensure your routine vaccinations are up to date. Check with your healthcare provider about recommended vaccinations for travel, including COVID-19 vaccinations.

5. Outdoor Activities:

- **Inform Others:** If engaging in outdoor adventures like hiking or water sports, inform someone about your plans, especially if venturing into less populated areas. This precaution ensures that someone knows your whereabouts in case of an emergency.

- **Appropriate Gear:** Use appropriate gear for outdoor activities, including sturdy footwear, sun protection, and hydration. Corsica's landscapes can be challenging, and proper equipment enhances your safety.

6. Drinking Water:

- **Tap Water:** Tap water in Corsica is generally safe to drink. However, in more remote areas, you may prefer bottled water. Confirm with locals or your accommodation if tap water is suitable for consumption.

7. Insect Precautions:

- **Mosquito Protection:** In certain regions and seasons, mosquitoes can be prevalent. Use insect repellent and consider wearing long sleeves and pants, especially during the evenings.

8. Transportation Safety:

- **Road Safety:** If renting a car or using public transportation, adhere to traffic rules and exercise caution on winding mountain roads. Keep in mind that Corsican roads can be narrow and challenging in certain areas.

- **Boat Safety:** If participating in boat excursions, follow safety guidelines provided by operators. Ensure life jackets are available and worn when necessary.

9. Local Regulations:

- **Respect Local Laws:** Familiarize yourself with local laws and regulations. This includes adhering to smoking restrictions, respecting protected natural areas, and following any specific rules at cultural or religious sites.

Pro Tips:

- **Health Precautions for Outdoor Activities:** If engaging in outdoor pursuits, carry a basic first aid kit, sunblock, and any necessary medications. Consider the physical demands of activities and plan accordingly.

- **Emergency Contacts:** Save emergency contact numbers, including the nearest embassy or consulate, in your phone. Share your travel itinerary and emergency contacts with a trusted friend or family member.

Prioritizing your health and safety ensures that you can fully enjoy Corsica's natural beauty and cultural treasures. By being prepared and informed, you'll create a secure foundation for a memorable and worry-free visit to this captivating Mediterranean island.

Language Basics: Useful Phrases for Travelers

While many Corsicans speak French and, to some extent, English, learning a few basic phrases in the local language can enhance your travel experience and foster connections with the island's residents. Here are some useful phrases to help you navigate Corsica with ease:

1. Greetings:

- **Bonjour** (bohn-zhoor) - Hello / Good morning

- **Bonsoir** (bohn-swahr) - Good evening

- **Salut** (sah-loo) - Hi / Bye (informal)

2. Politeness:

- **Merci** (mehr-see) - Thank you

- **S'il vous plaît** (seel voo pleh) - Please

- **Excusez-moi** (ehk-skew-zay mwah) - Excuse me / I'm sorry

3. Basic Phrases:

- **Oui** (wee) - Yes

- **Non** (noh) - No

- **Merci beaucoup** (mehr-see boh-koo) - Thank you very much

- **De rien** (duh ryen) - You're welcome

4. Asking for Directions:

- **Où est... ?** (oo eh) - Where is...?

- **Combien de temps pour aller à... ?** (kohm-byen duh tahmp poor ah-lay ah) - How long to get to...?

- **Pouvez-vous m'aider ?** (poo-veh voo mey-day) - Can you help me?

5. Ordering Food:

- **Une table pour deux, s'il vous plaît** (ewn tah-bl poor duh, seel voo pleh) - A table for two, please

- **La carte, s'il vous plaît** (lah kart, seel voo pleh) - The menu, please

- **L'addition, s'il vous plaît** (lad-diss-yon, seel voo pleh) - The bill, please

6. Emergency Phrases:

- **Aidez-moi !** (eh-dey mwah) - Help me!

- **J'ai besoin d'aide** (zhay buh-zwahn dey-duh) - I need help

- **Où est l'hôpital le plus proche ?** (oo eh loh-pee-tahl luh ploo prosh) - Where is the nearest hospital?

7. Shopping Phrases:

- **Combien ça coûte ?** (kohm-byen sah koot) - How much does it cost?

- **Puis-je payer avec ma carte ?** (pwee zhuh pey-ey ah-vek ma kart) - Can I pay with my card?

- **C'est trop cher** (say troh shey) - It's too expensive

8. Transportation Phrases:

- **Où est la gare ?** (oo eh lah gahr) - Where is the train station?

- **Où est l'arrêt de bus le plus proche ?** (oo eh lah-rey duh boos luh ploo prosh) - Where is the nearest bus stop?

- **Combien coûte un billet pour... ?** (kohm-byen koot uh bee-yeh poor) - How much is a ticket to...?

9. Expressing Gratitude:

- **C'est très gentil** (say trey zhawn-teel) - That's very kind

- **Je vous suis reconnaissant(e)** (zhuh voo soo-ee ruh-knoy-sahn) - I am grateful to you

- **Merci de votre aide** (mehr-see duh vo-truh ed) - Thank you for your help

10. Farewells:

- **Au revoir** (oh ruh-vwahr) - Goodbye

- **Bonne journée** (bun zhur-ney) - Have a good day

- **Bonne soirée** (bun swahr-ney) - Have a good evening

Pro Tips:

- **Practice Pronunciation:** While locals appreciate your efforts, practicing pronunciation can make communication smoother.

- **Engage with Locals:** Don't hesitate to use these phrases and engage in conversations with locals. It adds a personal touch to your experience.

Equipping yourself with these basic phrases will not only make your stay in Corsica more enjoyable but also demonstrate your respect for the local culture. Corsicans often

8. Corsican Treasures: Souvenirs and Shopping

Unique Local Products and Handicrafts

Exploring Corsica goes beyond its stunning landscapes and historical sites; it also invites you to discover the island's unique local products and exquisite handicrafts. As you journey through Corsica, be sure to indulge in these authentic offerings that embody the essence of the island:

1. Corsican Cheese:

- **Brocciu:** A quintessential Corsican cheese, Brocciu is made from sheep's or goat's milk. This fresh and creamy cheese is versatile, used in both savory and sweet dishes. Try it in traditional recipes like Brocciu Omelette or paired with local honey.

2. Corsican Charcuterie:

- **Figatellu:** A cherished Corsican delicacy, Figatellu is a type of liver sausage. Flavored with spices and often grilled, it's a staple in Corsican cuisine, enjoyed on its own or as part of a hearty meal.

3. Chestnut Products:

- **Farine de Châtaigne:** Corsica is known for its sweet chestnuts, and Farine de Châtaigne, or chestnut flour, is a key ingredient in many local dishes. Explore chestnut-based products like cakes, biscuits, and even chestnut beer.

4. Corsican Wines:

- **Vermentino and Sciaccarellu:** Corsican wines boast unique grape varieties, with Vermentino for whites and Sciaccarellu for reds. Visit local vineyards to savor these distinct wines and bring home a bottle as a delightful memento.

5. Corsican Olive Oil:

- **Huile d'Olive Corse:** Produced from the island's olive groves, Corsican olive oil is characterized by its rich, fruity flavor. Look for artisanal varieties that capture the essence of the Corsican terroir.

6. Immortelle Essential Oil:

- **Huile Essentielle d'Immortelle:** Corsica is home to the Helichrysum plant, known locally as Immortelle. The essential oil extracted from its flowers is renowned for its skincare properties. Consider purchasing this precious oil for its therapeutic benefits.

7. Corsican Honey:

- **Miel de Corse:** The island's diverse landscapes contribute to a variety of unique honey flavors. From the aromatic maquis honey to chestnut honey, Corsican honey reflects the island's biodiversity.

8. Corsican Citrus Fruits:

- **Cedrat and Corsican Citrus:** Corsica is famous for its citrus fruits, particularly Cedrat, a large, fragrant citrus with a thick, bumpy rind. Explore local markets for citrus-infused products, including jams, liqueurs, and skincare items.

9. Filigree Jewelry:

- **Filigrane:** Corsican artisans are skilled in the art of filigree, intricate metalwork creating delicate jewelry pieces. Admire and acquire unique filigree earrings, necklaces, and bracelets as timeless reminders of your Corsican experience.

10. Corsican Pottery: - Poterie Corse: Local potters craft beautiful ceramics inspired by Corsican traditions. From decorative plates to functional pieces, Corsican pottery is a delightful way to bring a touch of the island's artistry into your home.

11. Corsican Knives: - Couteau Corse: Corsican knives are renowned for their craftsmanship. These traditional knives, often featuring wooden handles and intricate designs, make for excellent souvenirs or gifts.

12. Handwoven Corsican Fabrics: - Tissage Corse: Explore the art of Corsican weaving with fabrics showcasing intricate patterns and traditional designs. Look for locally crafted linens, scarves, and home decor items.

Pro Tips:

- **Visit Local Markets:** Corsican markets, such as those in Ajaccio, Bastia, and Bonifacio, offer a treasure trove of local products and handicrafts. Engage with vendors to learn more about their creations.

- **Support Artisanal Shops:** Seek out artisanal shops and boutiques in towns and villages to find authentic, handmade products that showcase the skills of local craftsmen.

Bringing home these unique Corsican products and handicrafts is not just a souvenir but a tangible piece of the island's culture and heritage. Whether it's savoring the flavors of Corsican cuisine or adorning yourself with locally crafted jewelry, these treasures will serve as enduring reminders of your journey through this captivating Mediterranean gem.

Best Markets and Shopping Districts

Corsica's vibrant markets and shopping districts offer a sensory feast, providing an opportunity to immerse yourself in the island's rich culture and artisanal traditions. From bustling markets to quaint boutiques, here are some of the best places to indulge in retail therapy and discover Corsican treasures:

1. Ajaccio Market:

- **Location:** Ajaccio, the capital city of Corsica.

- **Highlights:** Ajaccio's market is a bustling hub of activity, offering a diverse range of local products. From fresh produce and cheeses to handicrafts and souvenirs, this market provides a genuine Corsican shopping experience.

2. Bastia Market:

- **Location:** Bastia, a lively port city in the northeast.

- **Highlights:** The market in Bastia is a treasure trove of Corsican delights. Explore stalls brimming with regional specialties, including cured meats, cheeses, and handmade crafts. The atmosphere is lively, making it an excellent place to absorb local culture.

3. Bonifacio Old Town:

- **Location:** Bonifacio, perched on the southern cliffs.

- **Highlights:** The Old Town of Bonifacio is a charming labyrinth of narrow streets adorned with boutique shops. Explore the alleys to discover unique items such as local pottery, handmade jewelry, and artisanal fabrics.

4. Calvi Market:

- **Location:** Calvi, a picturesque town on the northwest coast.

- **Highlights:** Calvi's market is a visual and aromatic delight. Stalls offer an array of Corsican products, from fresh produce to olive oil and honey. The market is an excellent place to pick up local ingredients for a picnic or to find unique gifts.

5. L'Île-Rousse Market:

- **Location:** L'Île-Rousse, a charming coastal town.

- **Highlights:** L'Île-Rousse hosts a delightful market with a laid-back ambiance. Browse through stalls selling handmade crafts, Corsican wines, and artisanal foods. The market square is surrounded by cafes, creating a perfect spot to relax after shopping.

6. Sartène Old Town:

- **Location:** Sartène, a historic town nestled in the Corsican hills.

- **Highlights:** Sartène's Old Town is known for its medieval charm and artisanal shops. Explore the cobbled streets to find unique Corsican products, including olive wood crafts, traditional knives, and locally produced wines.

7. Porto-Vecchio Shopping District:

- **Location:** Porto-Vecchio, a picturesque town in the southeast.

- **Highlights:** Porto-Vecchio offers a mix of upscale boutiques and charming local shops. The shopping district is perfect for those seeking fashionable clothing, designer items, and Corsican-inspired accessories.

8. Corte Craft Market:

- **Location:** Corte, nestled in the heart of Corsica.

- **Highlights:** Corte's craft market is a haven for those interested in traditional Corsican handicrafts. Local artisans showcase their skills with items such as filigree jewelry, pottery, and handwoven fabrics.

9. Propriano Waterfront Shops:

- **Location:** Propriano, a coastal town in the southwest.

- **Highlights:** The waterfront area in Propriano features an array of shops offering Corsican products. From boutique fashion to local wines and artisanal soaps, visitors can enjoy a leisurely stroll while exploring the offerings.

10. Santa Teresa di Gallura (Sardinia, Italy): - **Location:** While not in Corsica, Santa Teresa di Gallura, accessible by ferry, is a neighboring town in Sardinia, Italy. - **Highlights:** For a unique shopping experience, take a ferry to Santa Teresa di Gallura. The town's market offers a fusion of Sardinian and Corsican products, providing a cross-cultural shopping adventure.

Pro Tips:

- **Local Artisan Shops:** Explore smaller towns and villages for hidden gems—local artisan shops often showcase authentic Corsican craftsmanship.

- **Market Day Timing:** Check the market days in each town, as they may vary. Planning your visit on market days ensures a lively atmosphere and a diverse selection of products.

Indulge in the vibrant markets and charming shopping districts of Corsica to discover unique treasures that capture the essence of this Mediterranean jewel. Whether you're seeking culinary delights, handmade crafts, or fashionable finds, Corsica's markets and boutiques offer a delightful shopping experience.

9. Accommodation Guide

Types of Accommodations Available

Corsica offers a diverse range of accommodations to suit every traveler's preferences, from luxurious seaside resorts to charming mountain retreats. Whether you seek the tranquility of a secluded villa or the convenience of a bustling urban hotel, Corsica caters to various tastes and budgets. Here are some types of accommodations available across the island:

**1. Luxury Resorts:

- **Description:** Corsica boasts several high-end resorts along its pristine coastline. These resorts often feature luxurious amenities, including spa facilities, gourmet restaurants, private beaches, and panoramic views of the Mediterranean Sea.

2. Boutique Hotels:

- **Description:** Charming boutique hotels are scattered throughout Corsica, particularly in historic towns and coastal areas. These intimate establishments offer personalized service, stylish decor, and a unique ambiance that reflects the island's character.

3. Coastal Villas and Vacation Rentals:

- **Description:** For those seeking independence and privacy, renting a coastal villa or vacation home is an excellent option. Corsica's coastline is dotted with charming properties that provide a home away from home, complete with stunning sea views.

4. Mountain Retreats:

- **Description:** Corsica's mountainous interior is dotted with cozy mountain retreats and lodges. These accommodations offer a serene escape, with access to hiking trails and breathtaking vistas. Ideal for nature lovers and those seeking a peaceful retreat.

5. Bed and Breakfasts (B&Bs):

- **Description:** Corsican B&Bs are found in both rural and urban settings. They provide a more intimate and often family-oriented experience, with hosts offering local insights and homemade breakfasts. This option is perfect for travelers who enjoy a more personal touch.

6. Historic Guesthouses:

- **Description:** Corsica's historic towns and villages often feature guesthouses housed in centuries-old buildings. These accommodations provide a unique opportunity to immerse yourself in the island's history while enjoying modern comforts.

7. Camping and Glamping:

- **Description:** Corsica's natural beauty makes it an appealing destination for camping enthusiasts. Campsites are located in scenic locations, offering a chance to connect with nature. Some sites even provide glamping options for those seeking a touch of luxury in the great outdoors.

8. Agriturismi:

- **Description:** Embrace Corsican rural life by staying in an agriturismo, typically a farmhouse or rural estate. Guests can experience traditional agricultural activities, savor local cuisine, and enjoy a peaceful countryside setting.

9. Budget-Friendly Hotels and Hostels:

- **Description:** Affordable accommodation options, including budget hotels and hostels, are available in larger towns and cities. These provide a practical and economical choice for travelers looking to explore Corsica on a budget.

10. Vacation Apartments: - Description:

Vacation apartments and self-catering units are available in various locations across Corsica. Ideal for those who prefer more independence and flexibility, these units often come equipped with kitchen facilities.

Pro Tips:

- **Book in Advance:** Especially during peak tourist seasons, it's advisable to book accommodations in advance to secure your preferred choice.

- **Consider Location:** The type of accommodation you choose may depend on your planned activities. Coastal villas are perfect for beachgoers, while mountain retreats cater to hikers and nature enthusiasts.

- **Local Insights:** Engage with locals or your accommodation hosts to gain insights into hidden gems, local eateries, and cultural events.

Whether you envision a seaside escape, a mountain retreat, or an immersive cultural experience, Corsica's diverse range of accommodations ensures that every traveler can find their ideal place to rest and rejuvenate.

Recommendations for Various Budgets and Preferences

Corsica caters to a wide range of budgets and travel preferences, offering a diverse array of accommodations across the island. Whether you seek luxurious seaside escapes, charming boutique stays, or budget-friendly options, Corsica has something to suit every traveler. Here are recommendations tailored to various budgets and preferences:

1. Luxury Lovers:

- **Recommendation: Resort Le Revellata (Calvi):** Nestled along Calvi's coastline, Resort Le Revellata offers a luxurious retreat with spacious rooms, a private beach, and panoramic views. Indulge in spa treatments, gourmet dining, and upscale amenities for a truly opulent experience.

2. Boutique Charm:

- **Recommendation: La Signoria (Calvi):** Experience the charm of a boutique hotel at La Signoria in Calvi. Set in a historic mansion, this intimate hotel features elegant decor, a tranquil garden, and personalized service. Enjoy the fusion of Corsican hospitality and boutique luxury.

3. Coastal Villa Bliss:

- **Recommendation: Villa Bella Vista (Propriano):** For those craving privacy and sea views, Villa Bella Vista in Propriano is an ideal choice. This stunning coastal villa offers modern amenities, a private pool, and breathtaking vistas, providing a perfect retreat for families or groups.

4. Mountain Serenity:

- **Recommendation: Auberge du Bois Prin (Zonza):** Immerse yourself in Corsica's mountainous beauty at Auberge du Bois Prin in Zonza. This charming mountain retreat offers cozy accommodations, delicious local cuisine, and access to nearby hiking trails for nature enthusiasts.

5. Bed and Breakfast Bliss:

- **Recommendation: Chambre d'Hôtes A Muredda (Sartène):** Experience Corsican hospitality at Chambre d'Hôtes A Muredda in Sartène. This welcoming B&B provides comfortable rooms, a delightful garden, and homemade breakfasts, creating a warm and personalized atmosphere.

6. Historic Elegance:

- **Recommendation: Hotel des Gouverneurs (Bastia):** Stay in the heart of Bastia at Hotel des Gouverneurs, housed in a historic building. With its elegant rooms, central location, and proximity to the Old Port, this hotel combines history with modern comfort.

7. Camping and Glamping:

- **Recommendation: Camping U Farniente (Porto-Vecchio):** Embrace the outdoors at Camping U Farniente in Porto-Vecchio. This campsite offers a mix of traditional camping and glamping options, allowing you to enjoy nature with a touch of comfort.

8. Agriturismo Experience:

- **Recommendation: A Casanova (Sartène):** Immerse yourself in Corsican rural life at A Casanova in Sartène. This agriturismo offers a peaceful setting, farm-to-table dining, and a chance to experience traditional agricultural practices.

9. Budget-Friendly Comfort:

- **Recommendation: Hotel Cyrnea (Corte):** Budget-conscious travelers will find comfort at Hotel Cyrnea in Corte. This hotel provides affordable accommodations, friendly service, and a central location for exploring the town and its surroundings.

10. Vacation Apartment Ease: - **Recommendation: Residence Marina di Santa Giulia (Porto-Vecchio):** Enjoy the flexibility of a vacation apartment at Residence Marina di Santa Giulia in Porto-Vecchio. These self-catering units provide modern amenities and are conveniently located near the beautiful Santa Giulia beach.

Pro Tips:

- **Off-Peak Savings:** Consider traveling during the off-peak season for potential savings on accommodations.

- **Local Insights:** Connect with locals or accommodation hosts for insider recommendations on budget-friendly dining options, cultural events, and hidden gems.

- **Flexible Booking:** Some accommodations offer flexibility in booking, allowing you to adapt your plans based on changing circumstances.

Corsica's diverse accommodations ensure that every traveler, regardless of budget or preference, can find a comfortable and memorable place to stay. Whether you're seeking ultimate luxury, boutique charm, or a budget-friendly retreat, Corsica invites you to experience its beauty in a way that suits your individual travel style.

10. Conclusion

Unveiling the Wonders of Corsica

As we draw the curtains on this comprehensive Corsica Travel Guide, it is our hope that you are now well-equipped and inspired to embark on a journey to this enchanting Mediterranean island. Corsica, with its diverse landscapes, rich history, and warm hospitality, promises an unforgettable experience for every type of traveler.

From the sun-kissed beaches of Calvi to the rugged mountain trails of Corte, Corsica unfolds as a mosaic of natural wonders. The island's historic towns, each with its unique charm, beckon you to explore cobbled streets, ancient citadels, and vibrant markets. Whether you're an adventure seeker, a history enthusiast, a culinary connoisseur, or someone seeking tranquility, Corsica welcomes you with open arms.

The chapters of this guide have been meticulously crafted to serve as your compass, guiding you through the best times to visit, the intricacies of the local culture, and the wonders that await at every turn. Dive into the turquoise waters of secluded bays, savor the flavors of Corsican cuisine, and immerse yourself in the festivities of local traditions. Whether you're traversing hidden trails, indulging in water sports, or simply relishing a moment of serenity on a sunlit terrace, Corsica promises to fulfill your travel dreams.

As you navigate through charming towns, bustling markets, and breathtaking landscapes, take a moment to interact with the locals. Discover the tales behind ancient monuments, savor the warmth of Corsican hospitality, and relish the authenticity embedded in every corner of the island.

Corsica is not merely a destination; it's an invitation to connect with nature, history, and the vibrant spirit of the Mediterranean. As you explore its wonders, let the island leave an indelible mark on your heart, a collection of memories that linger long after your journey concludes.

So, whether you find yourself strolling along the azure coastline, hiking the untamed mountains, or sipping local wine under a starlit sky, Corsica invites you to embrace its unique allure. May your voyage be filled with discoveries, joyous encounters, and a profound appreciation for the beauty that Corsica generously shares with its visitors.

Bon voyage, and may your Corsican adventure be nothing short of extraordinary!